Chasing Shadows: Revelations of a Young Mind

A collections of poems and insights

By

Briana C. CaBell

ISBN: 1-4140-2812-1 (e-book)
ISBN: 1-4140-2811-3 (Paperback)

This book is printed on acid free paper.

1stBooks - rev. 11/05/03

To: "Aunt" Earnestine

Dedicated to those who thought I could and especially to those who knew I couldn't. For my mother and my grandmother. Special thanks to my 'Aunt' Esther: I owe you no less than my life.

What is greatness? The quality of friend that you have been to me. May God bless you with

PERFECT PEACE

2004

Briana CaBell

Introduction

I began writing in the second grade. I never thought much of it, it was just something I liked to do. I owe a lot to my second and third grade teacher, Mrs. Jenkins, for it was she who first turned me on to poetry. She introduced me to a world of words where everyone had vastly different opinions, yet everyone's views came together beautifully. It was through her that I discovered a man that inspired me to write seriously. The late, great Langston Hughes was then and now my favorite poet.

Several of my poems and writings have been called deep, depressing, genius, and even morbid. Think of these writings what you will, but remember that every one of these represents a different part of me. When I wrote each one of these I was feeling a different feeling. So when you turn each page - know that you are seeing into the window of my soul.

-Briana C. CaBell

Stop. Don't do that. Don't run. No trespassing. No turn on red. We are born into a world where limitations are so commonly put on our minds and freedoms that it is uncommon to find a person with no limits of mind. Think of the possibilities of such a person.

It was another one of "those" days. I hit my snooze alarm one too many times, had to wash up in the sink, almost killed myself putting on my shoes, and realized I was rushing for nothing because my clock was wrong. I'd forgotten to reset it the night before for daylight savings. I felt lower than a penny looking for change. I was hormonal to boot. I almost missed my bus and had to do a Florence Griffith-Joyner type move to try and catch my train that was just pulling onto the platform of the subway station and almost lost my nose when the door shut 3 inches from my face. I almost felt the conductor laughing at me. As I awaited the next train I noticed a man staring at me as if I was the last piece of bacon at an all-you-can-eat pancake breakfast. I tried to ignore him. It didn't work.

As the next train pulled up I was happy to lose him in the crowd and found a seat behind a partition so I would be barely visible and people would leave me alone. Lo and behold here that man comes trying to sit next to me. Now let me say I am a member in good standing of the BBC. The Big Butt Club. This guy must have been a founder. Note to all BBC members: **Two members cannot fit in one small subway seat!** Anyway, this guy proceeds to flirt with me like there is no tomorrow but forgot to remove his wedding ring. God, why is this happening to me today? I got to work and upon restarting my computer for the third time due to systems failures I glanced at a scripture I had taped to my upper cabinet. I really hadn't paid it much attention since I put it there, but this day I was drawn to it.

It says: For there is hope of a tree, that if it be cut down, that it will sprout again, and the tender branch thereof will not cease.
Job 14:7

A gentle reminder that this was just a day. And like a dead branch will be gone soon. When I retire for the evening the past is forgotten. When I awaken for a new day it will be just that: a new day. A new hope, a new beginning and another chance to sprout again.

Beautiful Woman

Look into my eyes
And tell me no

I will look into yours
And say yes

Look at my body
And say it isn't right

I will check the mirror
And say it is

Look at my achievements
And say they are not enough

I will assure you
That I am not through yet

Look into my heart
And say I can't

I will look into my soul
And say Yes I Can

Affirmation

I took a look at my skin today
The milk chocolate coloring
Silky, smooth and sweet
Tough, luscious and soft
I am a Nigger

My deep, brown eyes
No special color
Not green or blue or violet
They have seen oppression, repression and deception
I am a Negro

My plump, full lips
Spoken a lot of words
Laughed, scolded and shouted hallelujah
Eaten plenty of soul food
I am colored

Briana C. CaBell

My rough, coarse hair
Seen every style under the sun
Fried, dyed and laid to the side
Fro'd, braided, straightened and natural
I am an African American

My round, ample behind
It's been everywhere
From the jungle, to the back of the bus, to Wallstreet
Watch it as I turn and walk towards my future
I am Black

My Lord

Deep as the ocean
Hot as the sun
Low as the valley
He is the only one

High as the mountains
Wide as the sea
Cold as the glaciers
He died for you and me

Dry as the deserts
Blue as the sky
My love for the Lord
Never will die

You ask me how can I praise a God I cannot see?
I answer: You cannot see anything if you do not open your eyes.

Destination: Heaven

I'm packing my bags for a nice, long vacation
I'm leaving all my tears behind
All my sickness, all my sorrow
and all the pain I could find

I've been planning this trip for years
going to see a friend of mine
He's been waiting for me too
so I finally made up my mind

I didn't worry about losing my job
if I took too much time off
or running to the aid of my neighbor
every time I heard them cough

Maybe a few bills will be late
Maybe some people will give me flack
but where I'm going my debt is paid
and I don't have to pay it back

Looks like my flight is boarding
on the wings of a beautiful angel
over the rainbow and under the sun
I am ready, willing and able

Destination: Heaven

The Answer

I sit still among the willow trees
And hear the wind whisper my name
I glance up into the pale moonlight
To search for the answer that never came.

A wolf howls in the distance
As a signal to its prey
I look into the raindrops as they wash over me
And search for the answer that never came.

I listen to the pitter-patter of the little rabbit's feet
Scurrying out of the rain
I peer into their glossy eyes
And search for the answer that never came.

I think about all living creatures
And how we are one in the same
While I look into the misty clouds
For the answer that never came......

My Diary

A shadow of my world.
A description of my pain.
A piece of my heart.
A little of my soul.

Me and my diary
Very much the same.

The cover, like my skin;
Soft, smooth and impenetrable.

The introduction, like my eyes;
A mere glimpse inside.

The binding, like my heart;
Keeps it all together.

The pages, like my mind;
Never the same,

Always learning,
Growing,

The ending;
Indefinite.

Briana C. CaBell

Goodbye Song

She was so young,
so full of life.
Her heart knew not the meaning,
of worry or strife.

She never said a harsh word,
never shed a tear.
Yet I never really knew her,
how I wish she were still here.

She never made a promise,
she didn't intend to keep.
But she was never promised tomorrow,
she will not awaken from her eternal sleep.

She tried to help the world,
But in the end could not be helped.
The disease destroyed her from the inside,
Merely a shadow of her former self.

She won't see next Christmas,
or another bright summer day.
But of this girl we loved so much,
I can truly say.

She was somebody's daughter, somebody's sister,
and everybody's friend.
On this earth for such a short time,
yet her light will never grow dim.

Ignorance is not bliss.
Ignorance is the inability or refusal to learn

Red, White and Blue

When the streets turned RED with the blood of my brothers,
spilled senselessly, needlessly and unashamedly,

We were still Black.

When you felt your WHITE skin was superior to mine,
it was red in the summer, green in sickness and blue in death,

We were still Black.

When you looked at the BLUE sky and prayed for God to get
rid of us,

You treated us like animals, twisted Gods words to suit your beliefs,

We were still Black.

The land of the free,
The home of the brave,
Where were you when I was BLACK?

Eyes Are The Soul

The eyes are the windows
To the soul

The soul is the pathway
To the heart

The heart is the door
To truth

Without truth
We have nothing

Destiny

I am the master of my own Destiny

I walk the path that God has chosen for me

I am the master of my own Destiny

I wait for no man to open doors for me. I carve my own.

I am the master of my own Destiny

I am likened to a statue. Hard and unmoving.

Inside I am a child.

The world is in my hands. If I open my eyes.

I shall see my Destiny.

The only reality is that there is no reality.
Reality exists only if you create it.

Sweet Dreams

Close your eyes
little one

Don't see
your mother's tears

Cover your ears
baby girl

Don't listen
to her screams of despair

Purse your lips
little boy

Don't tell
how daddy hurts her so

Sweet dreams
innocent child

Fear not
tomorrow is another day

Truth is born of knowledge. No one on
earth knows the whole truth, the whole knowledge.
The only true knowledge is knowing that we
know nothing.

For you,

I shed a tear for you today

it burned as it rolled down my cheek

I thought of all the time we'd spent

in the months and years before

I shed a tear for you today

it tickled my skin just a bit

I remembered all the laughs we'd laughed

and all the cries we'd cried

I shed a tear for you today

it took a lifetime to fall to the floor

Briana C. CaBell

we whispered our secrets

and shouted our victories

I shed a tear for you today

we thought we had forever

never imagining we'd be apart

now that you are gone

i will never forget our time

that one tear glides over my smile

as i remember you

Another Weight

The drops of sweat pour off of my forehead
One

My shoulders slump deeply under the weight
Two

My knees began to buckle under the immense pressure
Three

How much more?

My hands tremble, my fingers numb
Four

My head pounds mercilessly, steadily
Five

My breath is coming faster, labored
Six

The weight of the world piled on my shoulders
How long can I stand?
One after another
More and more

Seven
Eight
Nine

One more and I won't be able to stand
Two more and I won't be able to breathe
Three more and my heart will stop beating
How much more can I take?

My Mothers Love

My mother always loved me
when daddy didn't care
She never let me down
My mother was always there

When I did something wrong
My mother made it right
She is my inspiration
My source of guiding light

No matter where I'm going
No matter where I've been
My mother will always be with me
Always my best friend

Briana C. CaBell

Memories

"A stitch in time saves nine."
my mother used to say.

"If your friend's jumped off a cliff would you?"
Daddy said.

"Money don't grow on trees."
that was Grandmothers favorite.

Granpop's line was: "Don't count your
chickens before they hatch."

They're all gone now.

"You never miss the water till the well runs dry."

Meditation

Taste the Darkness
Open your mouth wide
and let its exquisite texture
tickle your taste buds

Smell the Darkness
Breathe deeply
as the Darkness
invades your body

Hear the Darkness
Let its painful silence
Permeate every fiber
of your being

See the Darkness
Open your eyes
and see nothing
Close your eyes
and see everything

Feel the Darkness
Reach out
grab it with both hands
and pull it close

Be one with the Darkness
as it forces you to inside yourself
Let your senses be one with the Darkness
And love yourself

Pray For Me

pray for me

pray that my soul not be tarnished
with the injustice of my world

pray that my mind not go blank
with the thoughts of my communities hate

pray that my heart continue beating
despite the ignorance of my neighbors

pray that my eyes do not see
the despair of my peers

pray that my body withstand
The pain inflicted on me by my lover

i will pray for you my brother

Briana C. CaBell

The Greatest Love

He does not look at me with mortal eyes
He sees not my flaws or inadequacies

The confusion of my mind does not faze him
He sees through it to the deeper image

The words out of my mouth mean little to him
He listens to my heart instead, it never lies

He waves a nonchalant hand at the blood pulsing deep
through my veins
His love is deeper than the flow of human blood

It matters not where my feet have tread in the past
Only where he leads me in the future

My mindless mistakes are forgotten
He barely hears my sometimes-heartless words.

My lying eyes do not deter his unwavering love,
for he knows my heart.

It is pure.
As is God's love for me.

Briana C. CaBell

Love No Limit

Like the eagle that soars
in the bright, blue sky
Like the tears that flow
from my deep, brown eyes

Like the twinkle of the stars
on a dark, dark night
Like the snow that blankets
the earth in white

My love is like an endless stream

Like the vast curiosity
of an innocent child
Like the beauty of a flower
that grows in the wild

Like a candle that flickers
in the warm summer breeze
Like the steady drip of rain
that fills a thousand seas

My love goes on like a beautiful dream

Take from it freely
But give back the same
I will never leave your side
Just remember my name

My name is Love

My Best Friend

When you give your all
The Big and the small
You dedicate your life
And they give nothing but strife
Through the ups and the downs
Your love knows no bounds
When they turn you are there
When you turn they are where?
When she called you
in the middle in the night
When you helped bring his world
From the darkness to light
You sold your soul
And gave your heart
You gave every ending
A brand new start
But when it all
was said and done
You found that

you were the only one
Where was your friend
when times were tough
Where did you go
when you'd had enough
Where was she
when you needed an ear
Why wasn't he there
to wipe your tears
Well cry no more
Get on your knees
And look to the sky
The love of the Lord
will never die
He is your father, mother
best friend and lover
Above him you should
place no other
You will never be alone
in the Master's arms
He will protect you and keep you
from all of the harm

Remember these words
I say to you
Begin your day with a prayer
to start life anew
So when you need to fill
that empty hole
Just call on His name
He will heal your soul

The Graduation Theme

It's the end
It's the beginning

We move out
We move on
We move up
We move forward
We move to the future
We are one
We are ten
We are a thousand
We are infinite
We are doctors
We are lawyers
We are garbage men
We are teachers
We are daughters and sons
husbands and wives
mothers and fathers

Briana C. CaBell

Today we stand united
Ready to face the world
Tomorrow we stand divided
Ready to conquer the world

Lift your hearts
Lift your spirits
Lift your heads
Lift your voices

Be grateful
Be thankful
Be relieved
Be strong

Open the door
Your life is waiting

Breaking the Chain

Let the hardened links of racism
fall noisily to the floor

The hundreds of links of depression
rusted with defeat

The countless links of sexism
crumbled by the rise of women

The double hard links of emotional baggage and pain
disintegrated with the power of love

These links create an almost unbreakable chain
One of despair, hate and loneliness

With all the love and strength in your body
break your unbreakable chain

Briana C. CaBell

Pull, stretch and pry
until every link falls

Clinking, Clanking and Crumbling
to the ground

One by One
Piece by piece

Until you are free

To Whom it May Concern

I called your name even though I knew you would not hear.

I shared a memory with no one in particular and laughed in spite of myself.

I wiped away a tear because I refused to let it fall, enough sadness.

Sometimes I sit and wonder if you can see me where you are.

Are you thinking about me? Do you still love me? Do you remember me?

I've found that I am moving on with my life. I'm almost feeling good.

But just in case you were wondering; yes I still remember you.

Briana C. CaBell

Why?

Tell me why does all my happiness
eventually turn to memories
nothing left but fantasies
and i asked the Lord why
Why do i have to cry?

Why does the sun shine
for such a short time
everything seems fine
till i get caught up in the grime
and i wonder why
Why does happiness die?

So many beautiful colors in this life
but all i see is black and white
i try and try with all my might
but nothing seems to turn out right
and i think to myself when
When will the pain end?

A ball of confusion
An endless illusion
A terrible delusion
A continuing search for resolution

The world stands on it's own. Stars hang effortlessly. The sun and moon are one. I am but a human. A noiseless drop in an infinite body of water. What does that mean? That I am insignificant on this earth? Am I? Have my words touched you in any way? Made you smile? Cry? Think? If so then I am not insignificant. All we can ask of life and of ourselves is that we try to make a difference to someone else.

And The World Keeps Turning

A child laughs
A baby cries
A bus goes by
An old man dies

A careless whisper
A school bell rings
A robins' song
So many things

The rain stops falling
A rainbow appears
Still I am alone
With comfort from my tears

Briana C. CaBell

Revelation

The sun was shining bright that day.
Yet my thoughts were dark.

The children laughed and played outside.
There was no laughter in my lonely heart.

The music rang out cheerfully.
But my soul was silent.

I was lonely, sad and afraid.
I waited for a sign, and answer.
A flicker of hope to ease my pain.

In an instant I knew.

The sun was shining.
The children were laughing.
The music was playing.
I was alive.

Life is good.

Despair and Beauty

This is a story of the beauty that can come from despair.

A flower stands alone in a field, proud and unwavering. A beautiful flower indeed. All the other flowers had died off long ago. Some were withered by the sweltering heat. Some were washed away by the unyielding rain. All but this one flower. It held on despite having nothing to hold on to. Then one day tired, old, and useless the beautiful flower began to wilt. One of its large, colorful, fragile petals fluttered noiselessly to the cold ground. Try as it might the flower could not hold on. Every day its lovely petals drifted away and soon there were none to keep the flower up. It could no longer stand so proud and tall. It fell over. Dead. A vision of loveliness no longer.

But what's that? A sprout? The flowers seeds had taken hold of the soil and begun to take root. So, in time, the barren field was filled once again with beauty. Some withering away, the victims of circumstance but some stayed strong and proud. So you see, even in the face of despair true beauty lives on.

Surrender

No beginning
No end
Take these broken wings
And fly

No right
No left
Give your soul to the Lord
Never die

No up
No down
Open your eyes to the pain
Let go

No first
No last
Let love enter your heart
And grow

Nothing

Nothing but my tears
Being dried by the breeze
Nothing but my cries
Being heard by the trees

Nothing but my loneliness
Being the only sight
Nothing but my frown
Being seen in the night

Nothing but my sadness
Being soaked into the ground
Nothing but my heartbreak
Being the only sound

Nothing in the darkness
Nothing in the light
Nothing but my emptiness

Away

Away from the city

Away from the streets

Alone in the world

A lonely heart beats.

Away from the pollution

Away from the crime

In the still of the night

Immune to passing time

Away from injustice

Away from the hate

Briana C. CaBell

Never again to see

The light of another day

Away from the sadness

Away from the pain

A plunge into darkness

We are one in the same.

You talked me down when you thought I couldn't hear

You turned your back when you thought I couldn't feel

You cut your eyes when you thought I couldn't see

But I am clever like a fox
Quick like a cheetah
Strong like a bear

I am a mother
I am an earth goddess
I am a teacher
I am a giver
I am a woman

Briana C. CaBell

The Spirit

A glowing sensation
A wonderful vibration
An overwhelming stimulation

It started slowly, innocently
Spread through my body like fire
The joy, the excitement, the intensity

A lightning revelation
A stirring realization
A stunning pulsation

My feet started shaking
My legs had to run
I felt the praise in my heart

A beautiful elevation
A rousing exhilaration
A gentle, insistent purification

I felt the warmth in my heart
I breathed in the joy
Let out the pain

I am born again
I am free

Briana C. CaBell

Spring Cleaning

I cleaned out my closet today.

You won't believe what I found.

Several pairs of worn out shoes,

they've seen a lot of ground.

In a dusty corner

were some bags of tears.

Stored nice and neatly,

they've collected over the years

There was some jingling

from a box on the upper shelf.

Pieces of my broken heart,

too many to count by myself.

False hopes tucked under the frayed carpet.

A tarnished soul behind a too small dress.

A mountain of pain and fear,

hidden behind some unrecognizable mess.

Yes I cleaned out my emotional closet today.

Got rid of lots of stormy weather.

I haven't started my bedroom closet yet,

that's another poem all together.

Briana C. CaBell

Come Back to Me

I saw you yesterday, in my minds eye

I reached out with my fingers and traced your smile

I heard your laughter and wiped your tears

Till my memory realized you're no longer here

The wind whispered your name and I thought I heard your voice

Reality set in, such a disappointing choice

It's been a long time but I still feel you near

I know you're not there but your closer then you appear

Though the mind may wander and the soul may ache

The heart never forgets the love that was made

So one question remains maybe I'll never know

What do you do when it hurts to hold on, but you can't let go?

Not Yet

You thought you broke my spirit

Not yet

I thought I had no more fight left in my body

Not Yet

You thought my pain would bring the end of my life

Not Yet

I thought my back was against the wall, nowhere to go but down

Not Yet

You thought I was on the edge of destruction

Not Yet

I looked death in the face and said

Not Yet

I've been so low that the flames of hell singed my flesh

Not Yet

Many times I have stumbled and fell only to retort with the words

Not Yet

I have a lot of enemies left to defeat, a lot of burdens left to unload, and a lot of tomorrows left to live. So is this the end of my story?

Not Yet

Briana C. CaBell

One Day

One day the sun rose and blanketed the earth
in a sensual and radiant light

That was you smiling at me

When you closed your eyes to retire for the evening
the sun set and left a comforting darkness that wrapped
me tight

Your fingertips slid down my body
like warm, gentle raindrops that started at the nape of my
neck and ended at my ankles

My body shivered just a bit when your kisses engulfed me
like a soft breeze,
but your arms held me tight to keep me warm

Your presence hung over me like a fog
and your being seeped into my soul to complete me

We came together as one and our passion was like a tornado
the two of us wrapped inside each other destroying the obstacles in our path

You flooded my heart, shook my foundation and clouded my mind

Yes, one day you smiled at me and I fell in love

Never Forget

so it is with this tear that a love that

never was becomes a love never been.

take a bow for you have changed a life and

opened a heart.

look over your shoulder now and then for a

reminiscing glimpse of my face.

turn around and breathe in the wind

sometimes for a trace of my perfume.

listen in the night for the whisper

of my voice.

don't forget to remember that I am never too

far away to say

I love you.

Briana C. CaBell

9-11-01

I looked out my window this morning.

I saw two beacons of life and hope crumbling to the ground
in a cloud of smoke, tears and fear.

A single tear trickled down my face and I counted the seconds that it took to fall

when I heard the buzz of excited travelers
become screams of terror that barreled towards the heart of a nation.

My heart shuddered at the word's war, terrorism, tragedy and attack.

I hung my head as I watched America pick through the remains

of their brothers and sisters, mothers and fathers, sons
and daughters.

I smiled almost in spite of myself
when I glanced around at the resurrection of Old Glory
waving in the breeze and refusing to be choked by the
looming tension.

When I went to bed that night spent and exhausted
with visions of sugarplums replaced by echoes of warfare
I sighed to myself.

For I am an American

I am a child of God

When the smoke clears, when the battle lines have been
drawn and erased

When the sun rises and surrounds the nation with perfect
light,

When Catholics and Protestants, Jews and Gentiles
stand divided but fall united,

I will still be standing.

A bible in one hand, a flag in the other.

Peace in my heart and His word on my tongue.

Psalms Of The Negro

(Adapted from Psalms 23)

The Lord watches over me

Your whips and chains shall not break me

He helps me find peace in the field and

helps me wash the blood from my body in the river.

He restores my soul when my body is broken

He leads me down the path of freedom for the sake of my

spirit

Even though the master tries to kill me,

I will not fear his weapons for the Savior is with me.

There is always food on my table

Even though the master only throws me unwanted meats.

My cup is full with water.

He has mercy on me on the earth

and a place for me in Heaven.

Amen.

Diary of a Dreamer

Watching the clouds creep by, they know no sorrow, joy or passage of time. They just float in the infinite sky. Separating the flesh of the earth from the stillness of the heavens; eternal freedom. Free to chase dreams and condemn reality. Endless time replaces timeless ends. One cloud in the sky, one drop in the ocean, one moment in time. Seems like forever. You might say I've wasted a whole day starin' into space. Maybe I have wasted a day. But I haven't wasted a dream.

Lifeblood

I'm living on the far side of time.
Beyond seconds, beyond minutes, beyond hours.
A spirit swells deep under my flesh.
Building dreams, hope and love.

I'm standing on the edge of tomorrow.
Every grain of sand drips slowly, lazily from the hourglass.
Each drip reminds me of where I've been,
where I am going.

I'm sitting on the sidelines of reality.
Eternal life brings forth eminent death.
A death as swift as an eclipse and an afterlife
as long as the reach of God.

I'm breathing in the stillness of eternity.
Feeling the joy of my everlasting freedom.
A smile as wide as heavens, a happiness as deep as the rivers,
a love as free as time.

The Lady

I would liken the room to a night without stars,
until she arrives.
You can hear it in her talk
and see it in her walk.

She commands attention with her presence,
warms your heart with her smile,
and illuminates the dimness with her eyes.

She is fierce.

I would liken my life to a sleep without dreams,
until she touched me.
She helped my heart to heal
by showing me what was real.

Her beauty is like thunder,
intimidating to some,
awe-inspiring to others.

She is extreme.

I would liken this world to a song without a melody,
were it not for her grace,
filling this Holy place.

Her soul is as refreshing as a spring rain.
Full of the Holy Spirit, of love, of life.
She is simply......

The Lady.

Love Letters

If you get this message
I just wanted to say
I'm sorry I haven't called
But I missed you yesterday

When I opened my eyes
and realized I was alone
I started to think
of what made a house a home

The candlelight dinners
The countless tears
The echoes of laughter
The wasted years

The times that we shouted
The times we kissed
The times we said I love you
You are truly missed

You chair remains unoccupied
Your side of the bed stays cold
No one to talk to
No one to hold

So I got up the courage this morning
and picked up this pen to write
Just wanted to say I love you
Are you thinking of me tonight?

Broken Hearted

Tears roll down his cheeks like rain
A reminder to his constant pain

He rests his weary body upon his bed
A jumble of thoughts crowd his heavy head

He tosses and turns in his restless sleep
He may never awaken from his slumber so deep

The hollowness of his empty life
Cuts through his reality like a knife

His heart beats faster and faster still
The torture of his loneliness breaking his will

His future will never come
His tomorrow and yesterday done

Briana C. CaBell

The morning light shines on his sleeping face
Crowding itself into this stinking place

His eyes open slowly, almost afraid
Wondering if he can make it through another day

Afterlife

I find it hard to believe that forever never lasts that long.

Tomorrow never seems as long as yesterday and your
glad it all just fades away.

Today feels like it will never end when your enemies seem
better than your friends.

History is always repeating itself and reality puts your
dreams on the shelf.

The future sounds like it's so far off-line till you wonder if
it's even worth your time.

Forever seems more like a state of mind, when one year
feels like a thousand lifetimes.

But when you close your eyes for that eternal sleep,
that's when forever and reality really become deep

Last Night I Cried

Last night I cried
Because I wasted all my years

Last night I cried
Because He wiped away my tears

Last night I cried
From the fear I felt inside

Last night I cried
Because in Him I can abide

Last night I cried
Because the pain tore me apart

Last night I cried
Because He opened up my heart

Last night I cried
When He washed my sins, and took me in, and I'm brave enough to love again

Last night I cried
Because I'll never leave till my soul receives everything He has for me

Last night I cried
The tears were joy and pain, happiness and disdain.
They cleansed my soul and filled my hole.

He washed all my hurt away from me last night.

On Sunday

I opened my mind on a Sunday
You opened my heart on a Monday

On Sunday I felt my life slipping away
On Monday you told me it would be okay

On Sunday my whole world was crashing down
On Monday you help me turned my world around

On Sunday I'd just about given up hope
On Monday you taught me how to cope

On Sunday I didn't know what to do
On Monday you cared enough to see me through

On Sunday I couldn't see my way out
On Monday you showed me what life is really about

On Monday if I didn't show you enough gratitude
I'll spend the rest of my days making you feel valued

Until Today

Seems like just when you think you've learned the game
Somebody changed the rules

And when you try to build your future
You don't have the right kind of tools

So I'm here to tell you now
The word of God is real

His word is everlasting and unchanging
He will help your heart to heal

Until today you couldn't see your way
And everyday was just another day
Didn't know what you should do or say
But all that changed today

Just when you thought your hope was gone away
All that changed today

Did you know that someone cares for you
and will never let you fall?

God will always be true to you
and will never let you fall

Until today you couldn't cope
But God reached out to give you hope
All your pain came down like rain
But all that changed today

Just when you thought your hope was gone away
All that changed today

To Angel,

The pain cut through my heart
Like a flash in the night
You enveloped me in love
Told me things would be alright

Your beauty matches that
of an eagle in flight
An angel bathed
in a radiant white light

Through my every trial
and every plight
In my darkest of night
You were the brightest of white

Through every spot
No matter how tight
You pulled me out
With all your might

When I was blind
You gave me sight
When I was grounded
You gave me flight

I've done many things wrong
in the span of my life
But having you as my best friend
is always a right

Soul of Satan

When I look into your eyes,
I see hidden truths and broken lies.

Your words of deception echo in my ears,
supporting my pain and provoking my tears.

You used your web to tangle my mind
and made sure my happiness was hard to find

It took me awhile, but I knew from the start,
that you can never have a piece of my heart.

The eyes may be blinded, the ears may not hear,
the mind may be distorted but my heart never fears.

Rearview

I allowed my mind to slip into a memory but the salt of my
tears washed it away.

I saw my past in a dream of tomorrow and remembered all
the pains of yesterday.

All the time that I spent down, seems almost like a waste
of years.

I shudder at the thoughts when I recall to mind all the hurt
and fears.

I came upon a road well traveled and reminisced of paths
often chosen.

Wishing I could turn back the hand on the clock but the
minute and second hands seem almost frozen.

I try to remind myself it's not as bad as it seems, because
I'll never let the past overshadow my dreams.

A Woman Scorned

You let me down just one too many times.
Now all you can do is reminisce on my smile.

Remember how we used to cherish? Love, honor and obey?
When that other woman came you took all that away.

All those nights I prayed and cried,
but continued to stay by your side.

When the house was dirty and the bills were due,
I cleaned it up and paid it off too.

I don't need you to raise my kids.
You may have helped make 'em but you didn't help train 'em.

They know you as daddy but you were never a father.
On their first days and graduations you didn't even bother.

Now I'm walking out the door. I know you never thought I would.
There's nothing but a perfumed shadow of where I once stood.

I hope your new woman can be what you need
Because from this moment on......

I declare myself FREE!

I Am

You might call me special
I call myself a Child of God

You may think I'm gifted
I think I am blessed

You could say I'm talented
I'll say I'm anointed

You want to think I'm just lucky
I know that I'm just sanctified

Go ahead and think me an overachiever
I will go ahead and continue to be a believer

You could say I'm cut out to be a great one
I say I'm cut *from* the Great One

I am a Child of God therefore I am special.
I am blessed therefore I am gifted.
I am anointed therefore I am talented.
I am sanctified therefore I am lucky.
I am a believer therefore I am an achiever.
Through Christ all things are possible and I am all things through Christ.

Shame

I'm always hearing the same line
People say they're keepin' an open mind
But I'm looking around town
We're bringin' each other down
Killin' and cheatin'
Talkin' down and mistreatin'
Everybody sayin' it's all love
Givin' praise to the Lord above
But nobody's willin' to offer a hand
To help out his fellow man?

Ain't it a shame?

We're all livin' the same lies
Dyin' to get high
Killin' the same time
Wastin' the same mind
Tryin' to save face
We come from the same place

You're my brother in God's name
My sister in same faith
Why you walkin' right past me
Like you don't even know my name?

Ain't it a shame?

We're all cut from the same cloth
Workin' under the same boss
But we're ready to fear it
Before we're even ready to hear it
We're lookin' into each other eyes
Cuttin' the same ties
Breakin' each other's hearts
Ready to finish before we start
We're family and best friends
And we can't even make amends?

Man, that's a shame.

Don't give up walkin' just 'cause you gave up shoes. There are so many things I am. So many things I want to become. Often I wonder if I will ever meet all my goals. Life is not an easy road to travel. But if you give up after taking a few wrong turns you'll never make it to your destination.

Inner Beauty

My heart is like a lighthouse
Shining through the fog
Illuminating, shining, radiant

My soul is like a ray of sunshine
Bursting through the clouds
Rich, full, brilliant

My mind is like a burning flame
Lighting the pathway of darkness
Bright, exuberant, shimmering

My spirit is like a bolt of lightning
Flashing in the midnight sky
Blazing, glaring, dazzling

My light shines from the inside
No walls, no man, can hold it in

Today, I am blessed

Have you ever tried to chase a shadow? It's impossible to catch. Why do we pursue the very things we cannot conceivably grasp? What haunts you in your shadows? What are you running from? To? Stop chasing and start receiving.

Family Affair

My best friends can't talk to their mothers
They choose instead to confide in others

But when I am going through worry and strife
I turn to the one who gave me life

My mothers love transcends all time and never fades away
She helps me turn my darkness into a bright new day

I never have to worry and I never need to fear
My mother is my greatest ally day after day and year after year

What we have is special and what we have is rare
What we have is each other, a one-of-a-kind pair

Hallelujah

Hallelujah:
A simple word
The highest praise

Hallelujah:
A deep meaning
A deeper connection

Hallelujah:
When you're scared, alone

Hallelujah:
For the first, the last
The Alpha and Omega

Hallelujah:
For the answer to your question
The solution to your problem

Hallelujah:
An infinite blessing
for a weary soul

Hallelujah:
Such a glorious phrase
for such a glorious God

Hallelujah Forever

Amen.

The Girl Who Could Fly

She was a young girl, not very young. Rather wise beyond her years. She is inside us all. She was a sad sort of person. Not unfriendly, yet not really sociable. She rarely smiled, but nary spoke an unkind word. She loved her mother and had very few close friends. She approached life with caution, afraid of upsetting the people she loved. She tried to go with the crowd and was unhappy so she stayed to herself and was lonely.

It's a shame really. She wasn't ugly, stupid or poor, yet she didn't really have anything. The only thing she had - was a dream. A dream not unlike yours and mine. She dreamed of flying. Not literally, rather flying in the endless sky of happiness. The harder she tried, however, the further her dream seemed to slip away. She went to sleep with a head full of sadness and she awoke with a heavy heart. She was often reminded of a story she once heard, a story that seemed to have no origin. It had stuck with her for years.

> There once was a story of a butterfly. This butterfly had the most beautiful wings of any butterfly in the world. Wings that would have been appreciated the world over. This butterfly, however, was trapped in a jar with a tight lid. Every time the butterfly flew up he hit his head on the lid and fluttered back down. One day someone came along and took the lid off of that jar, setting the butterfly free. The butterfly was too afraid of hitting his head to try and fly away. He was free and he didn't even know it. He died inside that jar and the world never got to see his beautiful wings.

The girl wasn't sure why this story had stuck with her. It didn't make any sense. Surely it had nothing to do with her. She was a rational sort of person yet her dream never left her. The people close to her openly scoffed at her dream, which hurt her deeply. She tried to hide her pain but was successful only to a certain degree.

She guarded her feelings so tightly that she became physically and emotionally ill. She knew it must stop. In a battle between her head and her heart, her heart was winning. This girl, more of a metaphor than a being, with her head held high climbed to the top of the highest mountain and looked up. There was no lid over her. She finally understood. She spread her arms and flew.

About the Author

Her mother reflects that Briana CaBell must have been here (Earth) before because of her individuality and seriousness that appeared from an early age. One person commented that when Briana looked at you, you felt as if there was nothing sacred, nothing that could be hidden from the deep penetrating look she gave. Briana has initiated a poetry revival with works equal to those of Maya Angelou's *Still I Rise,* and Langston Hughes *Black Voices.* With ordinary words she carries the weight of her message. She speaks straight from the heart and soul. She has a lyricism learnt from her mentors, from life experiences, and a way of making the language in her poetry sing to any soul.